A Salute to Historic Black Women

D1069884

Copyright © 1984, 1996 by Empak Publishing Company

ISBN 0-922162-1-8 (Volume I)
ISBN 0-922162-15-8 (Volume Set)

Library of Congress Cataloging-in-Publication Data

A Salute to Historic Black Women.
  p.   cm. – (An Empak "Black history" publication series ; vol. 1)
  Includes bibliographical references.
  Summary: Profiles the accomplishments of twenty-four American Black women over the
  past three centuries.
  ISBN 0-922162-01-8

  1. Afro-American women – Biography – Juvenile literature. [1. Afro-Americans –
Biography.
2. Women – Biography. 3. United States – Biography.] I. Series: Empak "Black history"
publication series ; v. 1.
  E185.96.S244 1996   95-48498
  920.72'08996073–dc20   CIP
                                                                          AC

A Salute to Historic Black Women

EMPAK PUBLISHING COMPANY

Published by Empak Publishing Company
212 East Ohio Street, Suite 300, Chicago, IL 60611

Publisher: Richard L. Green
Editor: Dorothy M. Love
Researcher: Dorothy M. Love and Al Boswell
Production: Dickinson & Associates, Inc.
Illustration: S. Gaston Dobson
Foreword: Jewel Lafontant, Atty.

MY LAST WILL AND TESTAMENT

If I have a legacy to leave my people, it is
my philosophy of living and serving.

Here, Then, is My Legacy...

I leave you love. Love builds.
It is positive and helpful.

I leave you hope. Yesterday, our ancestors
endured the degradation of slavery, yet they
retained their dignity.

I leave you the challenge of developing
confidence in one another. This kind of
confidence will aid the economic rise of
the race by bringing together the pennies
and dollars of our people and ploughing them
into useful channels.

I leave you thirst for education. Knowledge
is the prime need of the hour.

I leave you a respect for the uses of power. Power,
intelligently directed, can lead to more freedom.

I leave you faith. Faith in God is the greatest power,
but great, too, is faith in oneself.

I leave you racial dignity. I want Negroes to
maintain their human dignity at all costs.

I leave you a desire to live harmoniously
with your fellow man.

I leave you, finally, a responsibility to our
young people. The world around us really belongs to
youth for youth will take over its
future management.

Mary McLeod Bethune

FOREWORD

On behalf of Empak Publishing Company, I am privileged to endorse the first in a special series of Black History Month publications: *"A Salute to Black Historic Women,"* produced by Empak. This booklet gives recognition to twenty-four Black women who pioneered and played a vital role in Blacks' overall struggle to obtain freedom, justice and advancement in our society. America, in general, is truly indebted to these Black women for their past achievements and fortitude.

Reviewing the lives and highlights of the women featured in *"A Salute to Historic Black Women,"* and familiarizing myself with the obstacles in their paths has reminded me of the continuing struggle that challenges our survival. Without their efforts, our development, as a people, would have been severely impeded.

For me, their lives are an inspiration. They struggled; they persevered. They fought against difficult odds to obtain their desired goals. *"A Salute to Historic Black Women"* is important. It brings into focus the fact that success is possible: a fact that should always remain in the forefront of our daily existence.

"A Salute to Historic Black Women" is an educational asset that any individual or organization will surely find beneficial. This booklet gives me a confirmed sense of pride, and I am grateful that these high-spirited and strong-willed women are a part of our heritage. I commend Empak Publishing Company for affording you and me the opportunity to reacquaint ourselves with their endeavors in *"A Salute to Historic Black Women."*

Jewel Lafontant

Editors Note: In her own right, Jewel Lafontant has also made significant contributions to Black America. Her extensive list of achievements include senior partner with the prestigious law firm—Vedder, Price, Kaufman & Kammholz (Chicago), board member to seven major corporations, and the first woman to have served as Deputy U.S. Solicitor Attorney General.

CONTENTS

Editor's Note: Due to this booklet's space limitations, some facts on the lives of the above noted Historic Black Women have been omitted.

IDA B. WELLS BARNETT
1862-1931

Ida B. Wells Barnett was a co-founder of the NAACP, an anti-lynch crusader and a most courageous Black woman journalist. She was born of slave parents in Holly Springs, Mississippi in 1862. At age fourteen, she was orphaned by a yellow fever epidemic. Despite this adversity, she managed to attend Rust College and Fisk University.

From 1884 to 1891, Ida B. Wells taught segregated public school in Memphis, Tennessee, and began writing articles for the *Free Speech,* a Black newspaper. In 1891, the Memphis Board of Education fired her because her articles were too fiery and controversial. Later, she acquired a partnership in the *Free Speech,* became its editor and traveled throughout the southern states.

Ida B. Wells was strong-willed and spirited. Once when asked to leave the "White section" of a train, she flatly refused and had to be forcibly removed by three conductors. She sued and won $500 in damages, but the decision was later reversed. She became an outspoken antagonist against the senseless murders (i.e., lynchings) of Blacks. When a friend, Thomas Moss, and two other Black businessmen were lynched for defending their property, she wrote an editorial identifying the murderers and demanded that they be brought to justice.

Later, writing under a pen name "Iola," she published a shocking, detailed expose' on the activities of the lynch mobs. The same night the exposé appeared in the *Free Speech,* her printing office was vandalized and all the equipment and copies of the *Free Speech* were destroyed. She went to New York where she joined the staff of the *New York Age,* edited by T. Thomas Fortune, and began a fervent crusade against lynching. She made several trips to Europe to publicize the facts about lynching. Her speeches were well-covered by English newspapers, which drew villainous attacks from White newspapers in the United States.

In 1895, Ida B. Wells published "A Red Record," a serious statistical treatment of tragic lynchings in the United States, which could not be refuted. She discredited the myth that Black men were lynched because they raped White women. The fact was, she stated, "they were murdered," as were her friends, because Whites felt that Blacks were "too uppity and too successful." In her appeal to President William McKinley for support, she stated, "Nowhere in the civilized world, save in the United States, do men go out in bands of fifty to five thousand, to hunt down, shoot, hang or burn to death, a single individual, unarmed and absolutely powerless."

In 1895, Ida married Ferdinard Barnett, an attorney and a Chicago newspaper owner, and later bore four children. Together, they used their newspaper to expose injustice perpetrated against Blacks. Mrs. Barnett became frustrated that violence against Blacks was growing and that nothing was being done. Once, when investigating a lynching in Cairo, Illinois, she found the Black townspeople too afraid to protest. Alone, she went to the State House in Springfield to argue against the reinstatement of the sheriff who had permitted the murder. For more than a day, she pleaded her case against the best lawyers in southern Illinois and won. That was the last of lynching in the state of Illinois.

Ida B. Wells Barnett was perhaps the most famous Black female journalist of her time. She was a correspondent for the *Memphis Watchman, Detroit Plain Dealer, Indianapolis World,* and the *Little Rock Sun,* to name a few. Mr. T. Thomas Fortune, a noted Black editor of the time, said, "She has become famous as one of the few of our women who handle a goose quill, with diamond point, as easily as any man in the newspaper work." Mrs. Barnett was cited as one of the 25 outstanding women in Chicago's history, and one of its housing projects bears her name. She died in 1931.

MARY JANE McLEOD BETHUNE
1875-1955

Mary Jane Mcleod Bethune has left her mark indelibly printed upon the walls of time as an outstanding educator, a giant of race relations, advisor to U.S. presidents, and the first Black woman in the United States to establish a school that became a four-year accredited college.

Mary was born to slave parents, Sam and Patsy McLeod, in Mayesville, South Carolina in 1875. Of 17 children, only she was born this side of slavery. She was a pillar of strength with perpetual drive and force. By courage, faith and perseverance, she was able to elevate herself to a respected position.

This great woman came from the humblest of backgrounds. She raised herself from the cotton fields of South Carolina to the position of White House advisor. As a child, she had a strong desire for knowledge, but there were no schools in Mayesville. It was not until she reached age 11 that a school opened some five miles from her home, and she walked the distance daily. After graduation, she was awarded a small scholarship by a White woman in Denver, Colorado, who wanted to help one Black child attain more education. Mary was selected and went on to attend Scotia Seminary in Concord, North Carolina, where she graduated in 1893.

Because Mary Bethune longed to become a missionary to Africa, she journeyed to Chicago, Illinois to study at the Moody Bible Institute. As soon as she graduated, she went to New York to ask the Presbyterian Board of Missions for a position in Africa. The Mission Board felt that she was too young and told her there was no opening at the time. "The greatest disappointment of my life," she described it; "those were cruel days." She later accepted a teaching position and married Albertus Bethune. The couple had a son, Albert.

In 1904, with the ever-present desire to educate others and $1.50, she founded a school for girls in Daytona Beach, Florida.

Her student body consisted of her four-year-old son, and five little girls who each paid 50 cents a week tuition. Her school began in an old house near the city dump. She used a packing crate for her desk, and her students' chairs were salvaged from the city dump. Through difficulties too numerous to mention, the school slowly grew. The student body grew from an enrollment of five little girls to a co-ed institution which became Bethune College. By 1923, when Bethune College merged with Cookman Institute, she had a student body of six hundred, 32 faculty members and an $800,000 campus free of debt.

Primarily an educator, Mary Bethune became involved in government affairs. In 1930, President Herbert Hoover appointed her to the White House Conference on Child Health. Several years later, President Franklin D. Roosevelt appointed her as director of Negro Affairs in the National Youth Administration and his special advisor on minority affairs. She also served as a member of the "Black Cabinet." In 1945, she was a special emissary of the State Department of the United Nations Conference. In 1952, she was the personal representative of President Harry S. Truman at Liberia's inauguration ceremonies.

Mary McLeod Bethune, the daughter of slaves, has many achievements to her credit, and was the recipient of many awards. She was received by lords and ladies in London and Edinburgh. She was blessed by the Pope in Rome. Mary Bethune left a legacy to her people, that her philosophy of living and serving would be inspirational to those who share her vision of a world peace.

On May 18, 1955, Mary McLeod Bethune, champion of human rights, a woman beloved by all regardless of race, color or creed, closed her eyes for the last time.

MARY ELIZABETH BOWSER
Birth/Death Unknown

During the Civil War (1861-1865), many capable Black women aided the Union camps as nurses, teachers and scouts, while others fought on untold battlefields as Union spies involved in intricate works of espionage.

Mary Elizabeth Bowser served as a Union spy. Many accounts of her life are veiled in mystery. Exact details of her birth and death are unknown. She was born a slave on John and Elizabeth Van Lew's plantation outside of Richmond, Virginia. After the death of John Van Lew in 1851, Mrs. Van Lew freed Mary and the other Van Lew slaves. As a favorite slave, Mary was sent north to attend school in Philadelphia.

After the start of the Civil War, Elizabeth Van Lew, a southerner who thought slavery "degrading" and was openly sympathetic to the Union cause, organized a most intricate spy operation (Her mansion was said to have been equipped with secret rooms). Fugitives she helped, supplied her with pertinent information, which she would transcribe into cipher code and send through enemy lines to Union officers, including Generals Benjamin F. Butler and Ulysses S. Grant.

The time came when Mrs. Van Lew needed an intelligence agent in the home of Jefferson Davis, President of the Confederacy. She sent for Mary Elizabeth Bowser. Through shrewd scheming, Mrs. Van Lew arranged to have Mary placed, as a servant spy, in the White House of the Confederacy.

Mary, of unusual intelligence, pretended to be a bit dull and unconcerned. She would listen to and memorize conversations among Davis and his men as she served their dinner table. She would read warfare dispatches as she dusted the furniture. It is said that Mary would steal away each night to the Van Lew mansion to report the military plans she had heard. Mrs. Van Lew, called "Crazy Bet," coded this information and placed it inside false eggs or printed it on dress patterns. Through her network of agents, she passed this information along to Grant, who sent replies back to her in the same manner.

The Confederate President never discovered that Mary was the security leak in his household staff. However, he was advised that the enemy knew everything going on behind their lines "as if the most secret counsels of the cabinet were divulged."

Accounts of Mary Elizabeth Bowser's war efforts as an espionage agent were carefully hidden by Mrs. Van Lew, even after the war. A secret diary was buried in Mrs. Van Lew's yard. Certain pages relating to Mary's activities had apparently been ripped out by Mrs. Van Lew, in order to protect Mary from any reprisal.

NANNIE HELEN BURROUGHS
1883-1961

Nannie Helen Burroughs was a prolific writer, educator, and Baptist leader. She was also founder of the National Trade and Professional School for Women and Girls, established in Washington, D. C.

Nannie was the eldest daughter born to John and Jennie Burroughs on May 2, 1883 in Orange, Virginia. Her widowed mother took her to Washington, D. C., at an early age, in pursuit of a better education. She studied business and domestic science in high school and graduated with honors in 1896. She later became an accomplished writer and editor, and also served as President of the Women's Auxiliary of the National Baptist Convention.

After graduation, Burroughs had hoped to teach domestic science, but was denied a teaching position by the Board of Education in the District of Columbia. This denial spurred her to eventually start her own school which would give all sorts of girls a "fair chance." Disappointed, she moved to Philadelphia and became associate editor of a Baptist newspaper, *The Christian Banner.*

Later, Burroughs returned to Washington expecting to get an appointment, after having received a high rating on a civil service exam. Again, she experienced disappointment, when she was told there were no jobs for a "colored girl." Bruised, but still proud and self-sufficient, she took a job as office building janitor and later became a bookkeeper for a manufacturing company. She then accepted a position in Louisville, Kentucky as a secretary for the Foreign Mission Board of the National Baptist Convention.

In the early 1900s, Burroughs established the Women's Industrial Club which offered short-term lodging to Black women and taught them basic domestic skills. The organization also provided moderate-cost lunches for downtown office workers. Later, she started to hold evening classes, for 10 cents a week, for club members majoring in business. Also, during the Depression, Burroughs established and managed a self-help venture, Cooperative Industrial, Inc., which provided free facilities for a medical clinic, a hairdressing salon and a variety store.

In 1907, with the support of the National Baptist Convention, Nannie Burroughs began coordinating building plans for the National Trade and Professional School for Women and Girls, located in Washington, D. C. The school opened its doors, in 1909, with her as President. Under the motto, "We specialize in the wholly impossible," Burroughs sought "the highest development of Christian womanhood through a curriculum designed to emphasize practical and professional skills." Her students were taught to be self-sufficient wage earners as well as "expert homemakers."

Although Borroughs and Booker T. Washington had similar approaches to vocational education, at no time, during the history of the training school, did the curriculum emphasize vocational education to the exclusion of academic subjects. She believed it was her duty to see that an industrial and a classical education be attained simultaneously. A purist who found grammatical errors physically painful, she required courses on a high school and a junior college level that developed language skills.

The National Trade and Professional School also maintained a close connection between education and religion. Its creed, stressed by Burroughs, consisted of the "three B's—the Bible, the bath, the broom: clean life, clean body, clean house." Of particular pride at the National Training School was its Black history program in which every student was required to take a course.

Many honors were accorded Burroughs. In 1964, the school she founded was renamed the Nannie Burroughs School. And, in 1975, in recognition of her courage and wisdom in espousing education for Black women against the consensus of society, Mayor Walter E. Washington proclaimed May 10th Nannie Helen Burroughs Day in the District of Columbia. Nannie Burroughs died of a stroke in 1961.

MARY ANN SHADD CARY
1823-1893

Mary Ann Shadd Cary was the first Black newspaperwoman on the North American continent. She published Canada's first anti-slavery newspaper, The Provincial Freeman.

Mary Ann was the eldest of 13 children born in Wilmington, Delaware to Abraham and Harriet Shadd. Many runaway slaves took shelter in her father's house, and the evils of slavery were clearly impressed upon her at an early age. Since it was against the law to educate Blacks in Delaware, her parents took her to Pennsylvania and placed her in a Quaker boarding school, when she was 10. Six years later, Mary returned to Wilmington and opened a private school for Blacks.

Mary and her brother, Issac, fled to Windsor, Canada after the *Fugitive Slave Law* was passed. She began teaching. Later, her father transferred the entire family to Windsor, and they were looked upon by their White neighbors as a "fine colored family." Because there was a vigorous campaign to deter runaway slaves from seeking a refuge in Canada, Mary wrote a 44-page pamphlet, "Notes On Canada," listing opportunities offered Blacks. The pamphlet is said to have been widely read in the United States. At this time, Mary also recognized the need for a newspaper directed to Blacks, particularly, to fugitive slaves. She established a weekly, *The Provincial Freemen*. "Self-reliance is the true road to independence" was its motto.

The newspaper became very popular, and Mary frequently returned to the United States to obtain first-hand accounts for her editorials. Mary felt the need to keep Blacks in the United States informed about the true conditions in Canada and to further refute the lies being spread that Blacks in Canada were starving. She also wanted to make her voice heard in both the United States and in Canada to "acquaint the White citizens with the noble deeds and heroism of the colored American," and thereby justify Blacks' claim for "equal and exact justice."

Mary became an outspoken public speaker and was noted for her quick wit in negating the efforts of hecklers. She was lovingly dubbed "The Rebel" for her scathing denunciation of the evils of the day, particularly the institution of slavery. In 1856, she married Thomas F. Cary, of Toronto, and later opened a school which advertised "no complexional distinctions will be made."

When President Lincoln called for men to fight in the Union Army, Mary Cary returned to the United States and, on August 15, 1863, was appointed an Army recruiting officer to enlist Black volunteers in the state of Indiana. After the War, she moved to Washington, D. C., where she enrolled in the newly opened Howard University Law Department. Mary Ann Shadd Cary became the second Black woman in the United States to earn a law degree in 1883. She died in 1893.

BESSIE COLEMAN
1893-1926

In 1922, Bessie Coleman received her air pilot's license from the Federation Aeronautique Internationale in France, to become the first Black woman pilot.

Born in Atlanta, Texas on January 26, 1893, Bessie was the 12th of 13 children. Although her mother could not read or write, she managed to obtain books from a traveling library wagon twice a year, so that Bessie could read to the family.

Bessie was born with a driving force to learn and to better her position. She finished high school and wanted to go to college, but her mother could not afford to send her. Instead, Mrs. Coleman let Bessie keep her earnings from washing and ironing to attend Langston Industrial College which is now Langston University. Bessie's money lasted only one semester. Afterwards, Bessie went to live with an older brother in Chicago, Illinois, where she attended beauty school and worked as a manicurist at the White Sox Barber Shop. Although her dreams of college had been shattered, she was still an avid reader. She began devouring everything she could find on aviation. By the time World War I was over, she had made a firm decision to learn to fly.

Bessie's quest to obtain flying instruction in the United States was fraught with blatant prejudice for two obvious reasons; her race and her sex. But, Bessie Coleman was not to be denied, she met both obstacles head on. Persistent in her effort, she went to Robert S. Abbot, editor and publisher of the Chicago Weekly Defender, for help. After extensive investigation, he informed her that the French were more liberal in their attitudes toward women and people of color, and encouraged her to study French and go to France.

With the money Bessie earned from her manicurist's job and from a chili parlor she managed, she made two trips to Europe. She studied under the Best European flyers, including the chief pilot for Germany's Fokker Aircraft Company. When she returned from Europe, for the second time in 1922, she returned as the only Black female pilot in the entire world. In Bessie's mind, "what use is an achievement if it cannot be shared?" Her primary goal was to open a flying school to teach other Blacks. Since money was a problem, she began giving flying exhibitions to raise funds to open her school.

Her first exhibition, in 1922, was at Checkerboard Field (now Chicago's Midway Airport). Between exhibitions, she lectured on aviation in churches and movie houses. In Boston, she did loops over the spot, on the Charles River, where Harriet Quimby (America's first woman pilot) had been killed. Once, in her home state, she refused to put on an exhibition at a White school ground unless Blacks were permitted to use the same entrance. They were, but they were seated separately inside. Her first accident occurred in 1924, in California, while doing advertising for the Firestone Rubber Company.

At the threshold of opening a school, Bessie suffered her fatal accident. On April 30, 1926, she had been asked to give an exhibition by the Jacksonville, Florida Negro Welfare League. At 7:30 p.m., flying at 110 MPH, at an altitude of 3,500 feet, Bessie put her plane into a 1,500 foot nose dive and never came out.

A most eloquent comment on the life and death of the world's first Black woman pilot was made in the Chicago Weekly Defender on the 10th anniversary of her death: "Though with the crashing of the plane, life ceased for Bessie Coleman, enough members of her race had been inspired by her courage to carry on in the field of aviation, and whatever is accomplished by members of the race in aviation will stand as a memorial to Miss Coleman."

It is said that every year on Memorial Day, pilots fly over Bessie Coleman's grave and drop flowers in her honor.

Ellen Craft was noted as a "master of disguise." Because of her nearly White complexion, she was able to "pass," and with the help of her husband, ingeniously escaped from slavery — she as a respectable White gentleman, and he as "his" slave.

Ellen was born in Clinton, Georgia. The daughter of her White master, she was often mistakenly taken for a member of the family. This so annoyed the mistress of the house that when Ellen reached 11, she was taken from her mother and given to her owner's daughter as a "wedding present." Although Ellen was a favorite slave and the conditions of her slavery mild, the experience of being taken from her mother was traumatic. This horror remained with her when she met and married William Craft.

In December, 1848, William Craft proposed to his wife a most ingenious but dangerous idea. Since slaveholders had the privilege of taking their slaves to any part of the country, and since Ellen could "pass" as White, if she were to disguise herself as a plantation gentleman, she could assume the role of master and William could be her slave. William, a skilled cabinet-maker, had been allowed to earn money and therefore had enough for their escape. Each had secured Christmas holiday passes, which made it possible for them to start their journey without arousing suspicion.

They stayed up all night before the morning they were to flee, going over all details. Ellen, knowing she would spend a great deal of time in the company of men, suggested that William get a pair of green spectacles to disguise her eyes. Since she could not read or write, she put her right arm in a sling, making it impossible for her to be expected to sign hotel registers. She decided that appearing as an invalid would justify her total dependency upon her faithful "servant." A heavy poultice tied around her face would make it appear understandable for her not to engage in conversation, and to speak (when absolutely necessary) in a soft tone. When Ellen dressed the next morning, complete with top hat, her husband observed that she made a "most respectable looking gentleman." After cutting his wife's hair, they knelt in prayer. Upon arriving at the train station, Ellen Craft, alias William Johnson, slaveowner, bought a ticket to Savannah for herself and her supposed slave. The couple's trip north was set with many difficulties. When they reached Baltimore, they were relieved that the first leg of their journey was completed.

In Baltimore, the last slave city on their route, the Crafts had a serious scare when Mr. Johnson (Ellen) was asked by the ticket agent to provide proof of ownership for his slave. After fearful, but surprisingly firm protest from Ellen, the ticket agent, noticing that the passengers sympathized with the invalid Mr. Johnson, sent his clerk to tell the conductor to "let this gentleman and slave pass," adding, "he is not well." They hobbled aboard the train bound for Philadelphia and arrived safely, becoming known all over the North for their bold escape.

The Crafts lived in Boston for two happy years before slave hunters tracked them down in 1850. The Crafts fled to Nova Scotia and then to England, where they received the help of English abolitionists. In 1860, the story of their early life and escape was published in London. In England, the Crafts learned to read and write at a trade school founded by Lady Noel Byron, the widow of the noted English poet.

The Crafts eventually moved into substantial prominence and gained financial success through their own efforts, and later through the successes of their five children. In 1868, William Craft sailed back to America with his family. They bought a plantation in his old homeland and conducted an industrial school for Blacks. Ellen Craft died in 1897, and William Craft died in 1900.

CRYSTAL BIRD FAUSET
1893-1965

Crystal Dreda Bird Fauset was a race relations specialist and the first Black woman state legislator in Pennsylvania.

Crystal was the youngest of nine children born to Benjamin Oliver and Portia E. (Lovett) Bird in Princess Anne, Maryland, June 27, 1893. Her father was the first principal of Princess Anne Academy, which later became part of the University of Maryland. After his death, her mother held his vacated position until she died. Afterwards, Crystal was raised by her maternal aunt. In 1914, she graduated from Boston Normal, an integrated public school and, thereafter, taught high school.

In 1918, she traveled the country as field secretary for the YWCA. She developed programs for Black working girls and students. In 1927, the Interracial Section of the American Friends Service Committee (AFSC) engaged her for an innovative program designed to communicate Black aspirations. Her ability to speak with "fire and magnetism," and with vivid frankness, devoid of rancor or bitterness, made her quite a respected figure. She made over 200 speeches and reached over 50,000 people in a single year. In 1931, she received a B.S. degree from Columbia University, and married Arthur Huff Fauset, a Philadelphia school principal.

In 1933, in her continuing effort toward interracial understanding, Fauset helped establish the Swarthmore College Institute of Race Relations and served as its joint executive secretary for two years. In 1935, she assisted the director of the Philadelphia Workers Progress Administration (WPA) and also began organizing the Philadelphia Democratic League.

A year later, Fauset served as director of Colored Women's Activities for the Democratic National Committee. Because of her public speaking expertise and her knowledge of political affairs, the Philadelphia Democratic party leader urged Fauset to run for the state legislature. In 1938, after a bitter primary, she won in a district where two-thirds of the voters were White. After her victory she said, "My interest is no way limited to my race, but is universal."

Fauset's victory gained national recognition. On November 8, 1938, she became the first Black woman in history to be given a seat in the Pennsylvania State Legislature. While in office, she directed her attention to slum clearance, low-cost housing projects, and fair-employment legislation which would ban discrimination against minorities. In 1939, before resigning to assume the position of Assistant State Director of the Education and Recreational Program of the WPA, she received Philadelphia's Meritorious Service Medal.

In 1945, Fauset founded the United Nations Council of Philadelphia, which later became the World Affairs Council, and traveled extensively in India, the Middle East and Africa. She expended considerable energy and determination in her undertaking of public affairs, and is credited for helping initiate positive socio-economic changes for her people. Crystal Bird Fauset died in her sleep on March 28, 1965.

The fact that Ida Gray became the first Black woman in America's history to earn a Doctor of Dental Surgery degree, in 1890, was indeed a monumental accomplishment during her time.

In 1870, there were only 24 women in the dental profession in the United States. By 1880, the number had increased to 611; and by 1920, women accounted for only about three percent of the total dental profession nationwide.

Prior to the Civil War, dental disease was common among the free Blacks, but few White dentists welcomed Black patients. Nevertheless, a few White dentists existed that were willing to assist competent Blacks in obtaining training so they could treat members of their own race. After the Civil War, Blacks practiced dentistry in increasing numbers. However, lacking the finances needed for equipment and offices, many of these Black dentists became "street dentists," practicing on street corners and in barns.

Notwithstanding, Dr. Ida Gray became the first Black women to graduate from the University of Michigan School of Dentistry; the first Black women to earn a Doctor of Dental Surgery (D.D.S.) degree; and the first Black women to practice dentistry in Chicago, Illinois.

Ida Gray was born in Clarksville, Tennessee in 1867. At an early age, her parents moved to Cincinnati, Ohio. She attended Gaines Public High School, and it is believed that she received her early dental training while in school and working for Dr. Taft, an early advocate of women dentists. Dr. Taft, the only dentist in Cincinnati at the time, and the founder of the dental program at the University of Michigan, was the very same dentist who had accepted Lucy Hobbs, of Iowa, as an apprentice in his office in 1859. In 1866, worldwide, Lucy Hobbs became the very first college degreed woman dentist.

Upon graduating from high school in 1887, Ida Gray entered the University of Michigan Dental School, where the dental training consisted of two terms of nine months each. Upon receiving her D.D.S. degree in 1890, she returned to Cincinnati, where she established a very successful private practice for five years. Well respected in Cincinnati, it is reported that a newspaper editor said of Dr. Gray, "Her blushing, winning ways makes (sic!) you feel like finding an extra tooth anyway to allow her to pull."

In 1895, Dr. Gray married James S. Nelson, and they moved to Chicago where she opened a dental practice at 35th and Armour Avenue. In 1898, she relocated her practice to 3558 S. State Street on Chicago's south side. A young female patient of Dr. Gray, Olive M. Henderson, was inspired and motivated by Dr. Gray in becoming Chicago's second Black woman dentist, opening her practice in 1912.

Dr. Gray also became active in several Chicago women's organizations, and she was often singled out as an example of what Black women could accomplish. Dr. Gray's husband was an accountant and lawyer. Having fought in the Spanish American War, he also became an officer in the 8th Illinois National Guard unit. After his death in 1926, she married William A. Rollins in 1929, and changed her professional name to Dr. Ida N. Rollins, D.D.S. Mr. Rollins later died in 1938. No children were reported from either marriage.

Retiring in 1928, Dr. Ida Gray died on May 3, 1953, at the age of 87. According to historical documents, recorded on her gravestone is the epitaph: "Dr. Ida Gray Nelson Rollins, 1st Negro Women Dentist in America."

ELIZABETH TAYLOR-GREENFIELD
1809-1876

Elizabeth Taylor-Greenfield received world-wide acclaim as a most gifted vocalist with an "astonishing" range easily embracing 27 notes. Mrs. Harriet Beecher Stowe, the famed activist and novelist, noted that Elizabeth "sings a most magnificent tenor."

Elizabeth Taylor-Greenfield was likened to the greatest of White artists of her day, particularly Jenny Lind, who was referred to as the "Swedish Nightingale." Elizabeth's performances created enthusiasm and reception and was so great that she received the sobriquet, "Black Swan."

Born in Natchez, Mississippi in 1809, Elizabeth was reared in Philadelphia by a Quaker lady named Greenfield, whose name she adopted. After her guardian's death in 1844, Elizabeth moved to Buffalo, New York. Seven years later, she appeared before the Buffalo Musical Association at Corinthian Hall. Elizabeth then began singing to packed houses "...of respectable, cultured and fashionable people," observed the Buffalo Press, and was critically acclaimed for her vocal artistry. She frequently performed before government officials, heads of state, and visiting dignitaries in Boston and New York.

In 1853, Elizabeth went to Europe. With the aid of Harriet Beecher Stowe, she was befriended by the Duchess of Sutherland, who arranged many concerts patronized by royalty. In May, 1854, she gave a command performance at Buckingham Palace for Queen Victoria and was accompanied by Her Majesty's royal organist and composer, Sir George Smart.

Elizabeth returned to the United States in July, 1854 and, as usual, was well received by audiences and critics alike. She received favorable reviews from newspapers that were pro-slavery. As so appropriately stated by the *Provincial Freemen*, a Black anti-slavery press, "...not a few gentlemen and ladies conquered their prejudices and made calls upon the gifted vocalist during the few days she stayed in their midst."

After the Civil War, Elizabeth settled in Philadelphia and opened a voice studio. In 1866, she and her students performed at the National Hall, "Festival of the Friends of Freedom", sponsored by the Philadelphia Female Anti-Slavery Society. Elizabeth Taylor-Greenfield, the celebrated "Black Swan," flew to great heights, bringing honor to herself and, most certainly, credit to her race. She died at the age of 67, in 1876.

FRANCES ELLEN WATKINS HARPER
1825-1911

Frances Ellen Watkins Harper was an outstanding novelist, poet and anti-slavery lecturer.

Frances was born of free parents in Baltimore, Maryland, September 24, 1825. Her parents died when she was three and she was sent to live with an uncle, Reverend William Watkins, who taught her at his school for free Blacks. At 13, she went to work as a domestic, but she continued her education on her own. She had the privilege of using the library of the family she worked for, and while still in her teens, she began writing poetry. In 1845, her collection of verse and prose, titled *Forest Leaves*, was published.

During the early 1850s, Frances Watkins moved to Philadelphia, Pennsylvania, a free state, to teach school. While there, she was drawn into the cause of anti-slavery and gave it her full support, through her pen at first, and later as a most effective speaker. Her ability to address large audiences effectively made her very popular. She developed a keen wit and a flashing sense of humor and was referred to by a newspaper woman as the "Bronze Muse."

In 1854, Frances toured Canada, where her writings appeared in the *Provincial Freeman*, an anti-slavery newspaper. In 1859, her narrative "The Two Officers" appeared in the September-October issues of the Anglo-African magazine, making her the first Black American to publish a short story.

Full of emotional spirit and expressive feeling, Frances' subjects were varied. She wrote comically on what to look for when looking for a husband, the plight of being unable to vote, the joy of emancipation, and the anguish of being unable to save a child from being sold. Frances Ellen Harper published several books, but her most popular work was a novel, *Iola Leroy or Shadows Uplifted,* published in 1892, making her the second Black woman to have a novel published in the United States.

In 1860, when she married Fenton Harper, Frances curtailed her speaking engagements. But after he died in 1864, she returned to her busy routine of lecturing and writing. Immediately after the Civil War, she went South and spoke to former slave owners and newly freed slaves. It was her belief that the lives of both were connected and that one could not succeed at the expense of the other.

Harper came in contact with all classes. She went to the plantations, the cities and towns, addressing schools, churches, courthouses and legislative halls, often at the risk of losing her life. She was looked upon as one of the most eloquent woman lecturers in the country.

A joyous day for Harper was January 1, 1863, when Lincoln signed the *Emancipation Proclamation.* She exclaimed to her audience in a rising tone of incredulity, "Well, did you ever expect to see this day?" Frances Ellen Watkins Haprer died in Philadelphia, on February 22, 1911.

MARY EDMONIA LEWIS
1846-1890

Mary Edmonia Lewis was the first Black American to receive recognition as a sculptress.

Born in Greenhigh, Ohio in 1846, Mary's father was a freed Negro and a gentleman's servant, and her mother was a Chippewa Indian. Her parents died when she was quite young, and it is not known who reared her.

Mary attended Oberlin College (Ohio) and studied both Latin and Greek. Although the school did not offer art courses, it was at Oberlin that she conceived the notion of becoming a sculptress. During the fall term of her fourth year, Mary's college days were brought to an abrupt end because she was accused of poisoning two of her White schoolmates in January, 1862. John Mercer Langston won acquittal of the charge on the grounds of insufficient evidence. She later moved to Boston, the center of abolitionism and liberal thought.

In the square of Boston's City Hall, Mary first studied the statue of Benjamin Franklin. With renewed interest, she took in every fine detail of the marble figure. She experienced such a powerful conviction that she declared, "I, too, can make a stone man." She became obsessed with an unrelenting drive to prove her worth to the world. She worked exhaustingly and with frantic haste. She was introduced to Brackett, a leading sculptor, who immediately saw that she possessed promising talent. After critics pronounced her medallion of John Brown, an abolitionist, as an excellent piece of work, the energetic young artist was well on her way.

Her portrait bust of Colonel Robert Gould Shaw, a socially prominent White commander of Massachusetts' first Negro regiment, attracted wide attention and established her as the first Black American sculptress. Afterwards, she received the support of a well-known Bostonian family named Story, who helped to sell her sculptures and also encouraged her to study in Italy.

In 1865, Mary went to Rome to master her technique. She worked directly in marble and was noted for her exacting mastery of the neo-classical style. Great artists of the day came to examine and to praise the works of this young, self-taught Negro sculptress. She was befriended by prominently established artists and patronized by royalty. She achieved her greatest recognition abroad. In 1876, she returned to the United States and was the only Black artist to exhibit in Philadelphia's Centennial Exposition.

Mary distinguished herself with many noteworthy works. Her bust of the famed poet, Henry Wadsworth Longfellow, can be viewed in Harvard University's Widener Library. In 1870, she created a bust of Abraham Lincoln which is now in the California Municipal Library at San Jose. Other noted pieces include: Death of Cleopatra, Hiawatha, Hagar in the Wilderness, Forever Free (a marble grouping), and The Freedwoman of First Hearing of Her Liberty.

Mary Edmonia Lewis won, by the artistry of her own hands, the freedom to create and to achieve.

MARY ELIZA MAHONEY, R.N.
1845-1926

Mary Eliza Mahoney was the first Black professionally trained nurse in the United States. She graduated from the New England Hospital for Women and Children in 1879.

Born in Roxbury, Massachusetts, Mary was the eldest of three children of Charles and Mary Jane Mahoney. Little is known of Mahoney's life before her enrollment at the nursing school. Before becoming a student, she had been employed at the hospital as a maid-of-all-work.

The New England Hospital for Women and Children graduated America's first professional nurse in 1873. Mary Mahoney enrolled on March 26, 1878. Afterwards, the nurses' training period was lengthened and academic standards became more rigorous. Of the 18 trainees who were accepted for trial, and of the nine who continued, only four, including Mary Eliza Mahoney, received the coveted diploma.

Despite the hospital's strict requirements, 12 months in the hospital's medical, surgical and maternity wards, four months of private duty, as well as lectures and bedside instructions by a doctor, Mary Mahoney withstood the pressure and maintained an exceptionally good record. And, inspite the rigid trends of discrimination, Mary's excellence eventually paved the road for other Black nurses. By 1899, the New England Hospital had five Black alumnae.

Mahoney was small in stature and weighed less than one hundred pounds. She is said to have been interesting, possessing an unusual personality and a great deal of charm. She worked as a private, duty nurse, employed by the best families in Boston and nearby suburbs, and was praised for her calm efficiency.

She was a member of the New England Hospital's alumnae association and one of the few Black members of the American

Nurses Association. One of the problems which always distressed her in the early days was the fact that good schools usually closed their doors to Blacks.

When the National Association of Colored Graduate Nurses was founded in 1908, Mahoney participated with much enthusiasm. At its first annual meeting the following year, she delivered the welcome address, was elected chaplain and given a life membership. She became a regular attendee through 1921 and was extremely helpful in recruiting for the association. She was also a fervent supporter of women's suffrage. After the passage of the *Nineteenth Amendment*, she is said to have been one of the first Black women in Boston to register to vote.

Mary Eliza Mahoney died of cancer at the New England Hospital for Women and Children at age 81, in 1926. In 1936, because of Miss Mahoney's unstinting work in the field of nursing and in the organization of nurses, the National Association of Colored Graduate Nurses established the Mary Mahoney Award. This award is now given in her honor for outstanding contributions to intergroup relations by The American Nurse Association.

Nina Mae McKinney, the "Black Garbo," was the first recognized Black female motion picture star.

Nannie Mae McKinney was born in 1913 in Lancaster, South Carolina. Her family moved to New York and, when she was only seventeen, she appeared on Broadway in the Lew Leslie musical review, *Blackbirds* of 1928. King Vidor, a motion picture producer, saw a performance and offered her the principal role of "Chick" in his motion picture, *Hallelujah*. Thus, she emerged as the first recognized Black actress of the silver screen. The energetic leading lady was an overnight sensation. As the tempting vamp, a role purportedly written for *Blackbirds'* star, Ethel Waters, she became the motion picture industry's first Black love goddess.

Nina Mae received rave reviews for her performances. She became the epitome of the exotic sex object. Her creation was that of both woman and girl, struggling between impulse and self-discipline with an uncontrolled raunchiness. Metro Goldwyn Mayer signed her to a, then unprecedented, five-year contract.

Although it was said that she was "one of the most beautiful women of her time," and that she was "one of the greatest discoveries of the age," her success was short lived. MGM failed to develop properties for her talents and her option was dropped. There were too few roles for Black female actresses, and she was able only to get parts in minor films and occasional short subjects, or in the limited-released race pictures of Oscar Micheaux.

Nina Mae McKinney left the United States to tour the cabarets of Europe where she was often billed as the "Black Garbo." She sang in nightclubs in Paris, Budapest, London and

Dublin. In England, she appeared with Paul Robeson in the classic film, *Sanders Of The River*. Still, her great potential as a film star was never fully realized. Hollywood had not yet found a place for the Black performer. Nina Mae was the first of many Black actresses, of leading lady talent, whose career would lead to a dead-end.

Nina's last significant screen role was that of the knife-wielding antagonist in the 1947 film *Pinky*, which starred Ethel Waters. Although Nina's career did not soar, her initial portrayal of the sultry "Chick" became the standard for enticing leading ladies in the motion picture industry. Nina Mae McKinney died in 1967.

MARY ELLEN PLEASANT
1814-1904

Mary Ellen Pleasant was noted as a financial genius and the "mother of the civil rights struggle in California."

Although there is some question as to her actual place and year of birth, Mary Ellen claimed, "I was born in Philadelphia, August 19, 1814." She lived a mysterious life, and records regarding her life are full of conflicting accounts. However, all documents confirm that she went to California during the Gold Rush days and became highly influential and very wealthy.

Legend has depicted Mary in many guises; as a blackmailer, procuress, civil rights activist, and as an important financial backer of the noted abolitionist, John Brown. Whatever her real story may be, it is clear that she was a Black woman of unusual force and ability.

It is said that Mary's freedom was bought by a Mr. Price, who sent her to Boston to be educated. There, she became acquainted with William Lloyd Garrison and other prominent abolitionists. Also, she met and married Alexander Smith, described as a Cuban planter who, after his death, left her a substantial legacy of $45,000, asking that she use the money to aid the abolitionsts' cause.

About 1849, Mary and her second husband, John Pleasant, went west to San Francisco, where she promptly went into business. Mary Ellen Pleasant, referred to as "Mammy Pleasant" behind her back, opened and successfully operated a string of fashionable boardinghouses and restaurants. Among her boarders, it is reported, were men who became prominent business giants and political figures. Other accounts have her giving financial advice to many of her clients who, after taking her advice, enjoyed substantial financial success.

The business accomplishments of Mammy Pleasant in no way diminished her support of the Black struggle. She aided and hid fugitive slaves. She often made special trips to rural areas to rescue slaves who were being held illegally by masters. She challenged California's Jim Crow laws. She was instrumental in the passing of a legislative act in 1863, giving Blacks the right of testimony in court.

Mary Pleasant was especially active in establishing the right of Blacks to ride on the city's streetcars. It is recorded in California's court records and newspapers that she filed a suit bringing action against two trolley lines whose conductors had refused her passage. It is further alleged that she went north to Canada, in 1858, and donated $30,000 to John Brown to aid in the historic John Brown raid.

In 1904, Mary Ellen Pleasant died in the home of friends in San Francisco. Some say she left an estate, in excess of $300,000, to those who cared for her in her declining years.

FLORENCE BEATRICE SMITH PRICE
1888-1953

Florence B. Price was the first Black woman to be recognized worldwide as an award winning composer.

Florence was born on April 9, 1888, in Little Rock, Arkansas. Her mother, a music teacher, recognized her musical talent and taught her to play the piano at an early age. She gave her first recital at the age of four. Before completing high school in 1903, she had composed and published her first musical composition.

Florence attended the best schools and studied under the best professors. She attended the New England Conservatory of Music in Boston and studied under the noted George Chadwick, director of the Conservatory. Before graduating from college, Florence was credited with a composed, performed symphony. During a six-year span after graduation, she was married and taught at Shorter College in North Little Rock, Arkansas (1906-1910) and Clark University in Atlanta, Georgia (1910-1912).

In 1927, Florence moved to Chicago, Illinois and began teaching privately. Later, she studied at the University of Chicago, the American Conservatory, Chicago Musical College and Chicago Teachers College. Florence was fortunate. Opportunities for young Black artists were few, but she was able to earn money by writing radio commercials and publishing, for her musical scores. Her style was conservative for her time, she wrote in a neo-romantic style and sometimes drew upon Black folk music elements, using Black dance forms for her instrumental compositions, and Black poetry as lyrics for her songs.

Determined to make her works known, Florence entered one competition after another. In 1925, her persistence and perseverance proved fruitful. She won her first prize in the

Opportunity Magazine's Holstein Price competition for her musical arrangement "In The Land O'Cotton." In 1932, she took first place in the Wanarmaker Music Contest for her "Symphony in E Minor," thereby attracting widespread attention as the first Black to receive recognition as a bona fide composer.

The following year, the Chicago Symphony performed one of Florence Price's works at the Chicago World's Fair. It was the first time in history that a major orchestra had performed the symphony of a Black woman. Her success created grand excitement, and musical doors were opened for her across the Nation. The Brooklyn Symphony, American Symphony, Detroit Symphony, Chicago Chamber Orchestra, to name a few, began performing her orchestral works. Famous pianists performed her concertos, and celebrated singers, such as Roland Hayes, Marian Anderson and Leontyne Price sang her songs.

Florence Price left behind a musical repertoire classed among the best. She died in Chicago on June 3, 1953, after establishing herself as a worthy, creative Black American.

DR. SUSAN McKINNEY STEWARD
1848-1918

Dr. Susan McKinney Steward is reputedly the first Black woman to formally enter the medical profession and to gain recognizable success.

Although Susan was confronted with two major barriers, being Black and a woman, this highly self-motivated and determined woman overcame both successfully. She graduated from the New York Medical School for Women and Children as valedictorian of her class in 1870.

Dr. Steward was born Susan Smith in Brooklyn, New York, in 1848. She later married William G. McKinney, and bore a son and a daughter. After the death of her husband in 1894, she became an organist and choirmaster at the Bridge Street African Methodist Church and a board member of the Brooklyn Home for Aged Colored People. An avid student of the history and progress of women in medicine, she was one of the founders of the Women's Royal Union of New York and Brooklyn. She also served as an active member of the Kings County Homeopathic Society.

She did her postgraduate work at Long Island College Hospital and was further distinguished as being the only female in her graduating class. Early in her career, she practiced *homeopathy at a hospital and dispensary. During her association with the hospital, the dispensary practice grew in size and had to be moved to larger quarters. It was later renamed the Memorial Hospital for Women & Children. Dr. Steward also had a successful private practice in Brooklyn for more than 20 years, and she eventually opened a second office in Manhattan.

Later, after the death of her first husband, she married the Reverend T. G. Steward, a U.S. Army chaplain and instructor at Wilberforce University. Shortly thereafter, she left Brooklyn and made her home in Wilberforce, Ohio, where she practiced for many years. She died in 1918.

*Homeopathy: A system of medical practice that treats a disease esp. by the administration of minute doses of a remedy that would in healthy persons produce symptoms of the disease treated. (Webster's New Collegiate Dictionary, 1979).

ELLA PHILLIPS STEWART
1893 - 1987

Ella Phillips Stewart, was a nationally known Black woman pharmacist and a noted contributor to American life and international affairs.

Ella was born to Eliza and Hamp Phillips, sharecroppers, in a small town outside of Berryville, Virginia, on March 6, 1893. In grade school, she was always a leader in her class. She maintained this standing through college, and subsequently distinguished herself by winning five major academic scholarships at Storer College in West Virginia. After graduating from Storer, she married Charles Myers, a fellow classmate, but divorced him three years later. A daughter, Virginia, born to this marriage, lived to be only two years old.

Afterwards, Ella moved to Pittsburgh and took a job as a bookkeeper in a drugstore. Later, she was urged by a physician friend to enter the field of pharmacology. She graduated from the Pittsburgh University School of Pharmacy in 1916, becoming the first Black to do so, and further became the first Black woman to pass the Pennsylvania State Board Pharmacology Exam.

After earning her degree, Ella's held her first position as a pharmacist at a drugstore owned by two Jewish classmates. But, her ultimate dream was to have a drugstore of her own. She instituted plans and realized her dream. When World War I was over, she closed her store and took a position at the Braddock General Hospital for two years, and subsequently bought another drugstore.

In 1920, she married William Wyatt Stewart, also a pharmacist, and they moved to Youngstown, Ohio. In 1922, the couple bought a building for their new drugstore in Toledo,

Ohio, in a predominantly White area. There they served the community for 23 years.

Added to Dr. Stewart's career as a successful pharmacist is a vast list of outstanding achievements, distinguished awards, honorary degrees and citations. She has been honored with coveted community service awards and inducted into Ohio Women's Hall of Fame. In 1948, she was elected to a four-year term as President of the National Association of Colored Women (NACW) and authored its book *Lifting as They Climb*.

In 1951, Dr. Stewart was placed on the Women's Advisory Committee of Defense Manpower by the U.S. Department of Labor, and a short while later selected as a delegate of the NACW to attend the International Council of Women of the World in Athens, Greece. In 1954-55, she served as goodwill ambassador for the U.S. State Department and toured 23 countries for the Education Exchange Service. She lectured in such countries as India, Indonesia, the Phillippines, Japan, and China. In 1961, the city of Toledo named a $3 million elementary school in her honor.

In 1963, Secretary of State, Dean Rusk, appointed Ella Stewart to the Executive Board of the U.S. Commission of United Nations Educational, Social and Cultural Organization (UNESCO). The Ella P. Stewart Elementary School established a museum in 1974, which houses an impressive collection of artifacts collected by Mrs. Stewart during her travels.

Ella Phillips Stewart died on November 27, 1987, at the Mercy Hospital in Toledo, Ohio. Of her many accomplishments and tributes, she seemed to cherish most deeply the naming of the elementary school in her honor.

MARY CHURCH TERRELL
1863-1954

Mary Church Terrell was noted as a champion of women's rights long before feminism was popular. She was a writer, organizer, lecturer and an active demonstrator for equality, to which she devoted her entire life.

Born of well-to-do parents in Memphis, Tennessee, in 1863, Mary was sent to a private school in Ohio, and later to Oberlin College, where she graduated with a major in classical languages in 1884. The only woman in a class of forty men, she won recognition as class poet, member of the honorary literary society, and editor of the Oberlin Review.

After graduation, Mary took a teaching position at Wilberforce University, then sailed to Europe to perfect her language skills. After returning to the United States, she pursued a master's degree at Oberlin. The college offered her the position of Registrar, the highest position ever accorded a Black woman at a leading college. However, Miss Church declined the position to wed Robert Terrell (who became the first Black municipal judge of Washington, D. C.) in 1891. The couple had two daughters. The eldest was named in honor of the Black poetess, Phillis Wheatley.

Mary Church Terrell is credited with numerous achievements. In 1892, she helped organize the Colored Women's League of Washington D.C. A few years later, she was instrumental in strengthening the League's forces to form the National Association of Colored Women. The organization elected her president for two terms and later named her honorary president. The association's motto was "Lifting As They Climb," and its aim was to assist poor and illiterate Blacks.

In 1895, Washington, D.C. officials appointed her for the first of two terms on its Board of Education. She served on the board, until 1911, as the first Black woman to hold that position. She helped establish the Delta Sigma Theta sorority in 1913 and later wrote its famous creed.

Mary Terrell was active in the political arena as well, campaigning and speaking out against discrimination and segregation. In 1904, she acquired an international reputation in Berlin, Germany, when she addressed the International Council of Women. As the only American delegate not restricted to her native tongue, she addressed the Conference, to the amazement of the delegates, fluently in three languages: English, French and German. Although Mary Terrell interchanged her languages, her theme remained the same—equal rights for women and the Black race.

Not only was Mrs. Terrell highly educated and intellectual, she was extremely attractive. She used her inherited fair complexion to great advantage in her fight against racial injustice. Frequently, she would enter a segregated restaurant and, after having been served as a White woman, would demand to know why others of her race were not allowed to eat there.

Mary had found a copy of a law established during the Reconstruction days, which ordered restaurants to serve "any respectable, well-behaved person." Failure to do so meant forfeiture of license. She headed a committee of distinguished Black citizens to demand enforcement of this 80-year-old law. She and several other Blacks went to a number of restaurants and, after being refused service, filed a law suit which went before the Supreme Court. In 1953, the U.S. Supreme Court decided in her favor.

Mary Church Terrell fought what she considered a "righteous war" until her death at age 91. She died in 1954, just a few months after hearing the United States Supreme Court declare that segregation itself was unconstitutional.

SOJOURNER TRUTH
1797-1883

Sojourner Truth, born Isabella Baumfree in 1797, was a pilgrim of freedom and a fervent women's rights activist. She thundered against slavery from countless platforms. For nearly 40 years, she traveled across the country lecturing on the two major issues of the time; abolition and the rights of the "lesser sex." She was born in slavery to James and Betsy Baumfree near Kingston, New York.

Sojourner Truth was the first Negro woman orator to lecture against slavery. She wore a satin banner across her chest bearing the words, "Proclaim liberty throughout the land unto all the inhabitants thereof." Of how she came to be called Sojourner Truth she said, "I asked the Lord to give me a new name and He gave me SOJOURNER because I was to travel up and down the land showing the people sins and being a sign unto them. Afterwards, I told the Lord I wanted another name cause everybody else had two names; and He gave me TRUTH because I was to declare the truth unto the People."

Until the New York State *Emancipation Act* freed her in 1828, Sojourner was sold from master to master. About 1810, she was sold to John J. Dumont who forced her to marry an older slave, named Thomas, by whom she bore five children. Dumont, with little regard for human personage, heartlessly sold several of her children. In 1827, Sojourner escaped from Dumont and took refuge with a Quaker family whose name she took, becoming Isabella Van Wagener. With their assistance, she won a lawsuit to have one son, Peter, returned to her.

As a speaker, Sojourner was not eloquent, but she was tremendously effective. Her strong towering stature, over 6 feet, commanded respect. Her deep, bass voice commanded attention. Her acid intelligence and stern countenance created a sense of drama that hushed the jeers of even the worse hecklers. She delivered one of her most widely quoted speeches, on equality between the sexes, at a suffrage meeting in Akron, Ohio, in 1852.

To demolish the male argument about the helplessness of women, and to discredit her detractors' claim that she was actually a man disguised as a woman, she ripped open her blouse baring one breast and a muscular arm as evidence that she and other women worked just as hard as men, but did not enjoy the same privileges. She asked, "Ain't I a woman?"

This woman who could neither read nor write became famous as an itinerant preacher. Wherever she spoke, crowds flocked to hear her. She was a self-styled prophetess and orator, and it is thought that she produced some mystical effect on her audiences, whether at a religious camp or an anti-slavery rally.

Sojourner was indeed a legend in her time. Her work was not confined to anti-slavery and women's rights alone, but embraced all human rights that were being encroached upon or denied. During the Civil War, she raised money for soldier's gifts by lecturing and singing (many of her songs were self-composed); she also served as a nurse and helped resettle many slaves who fled the South.

The highlight of her Soujourner life was when she was received by President Lincoln at the White House. She was well into her seventies before she retired, due to poor health, from the battlefield of injustice. Her epitaph is taken from a well-known retort she once made to Frederick Douglass, after his deliverance of a rather gloomy speech regarding the plight of Black Americans. Sojourner rose and asked, "Frederick, is God dead?"

HARRIET ROSS TUBMAN
1820-1913

"Strong as a man, brave as a lion, cunning as a fox," Harriet Tubman was undoubtedly one of the greatest Underground Railroad conductors of her time. The Underground Railroad was not a real railroad, but a network of concerned people across the country who devised an escape route from state to state, promoting freedom for slaves.

Harriet, one of 10 or 11 children, was born in 1820, in Maryland, to Benjamin and Harriet Ross. During the eight years she conducted the Underground Railroad, she made 19 perilous trips in the deep South and guided over 300 slaves to a new and glorious life of freedom. Her undaunted courage and fearless acts earned her the sobriquet, "Moses of Her People." She was greatly respected in abolitionist circles in England, Scotland, Ireland and Liberia. Tubman received financial aid from Great Britain and Canada. Queen Victoria of England sent her expensive gifts and a personal invitation to visit Britain.

From an early age, Harriet was brutalized and compelled to do hard labor by her masters. All of this harsh treatment toughened her body and gave her unrelenting stamina which served her well in later years. When she was 13, her master struck her with a two-pound weight and fractured her skull. For the rest of her life, she suffered from attacks of dizziness and uncontrollable sleeping spells from which she could not easily be awakened.

In 1844, Harriet married John Tubman, a freed man. Several years later, her master died and there was talk of his slaves being sold out of the state. Apprehensive of her fate, Harriet decided to escape. Upon hearing her plan, her husband ridiculed her and refused to leave with her. Harriet responded by saying, "There's two things I've a right to: death or liberty. One or the other I mean to have. No one will take me back alive." Faithful to her promise, she made her escape through the swamps with two brothers who later were overcome with fear and turned back, leaving her to go it alone. No one ever turned back on her again. She carried a rifle for protection and also to instill courage and motivation into the spirits of her sometime faltering charges who felt they couldn't go on. At such times, she would point her gun and quietly command, "You'll be free, or you will die." She is noted for saying, "I never ran my train off the track and I never lost a passenger."

It was dangerous for anyone to help "property" escape— even more so for Harriet, a slave herself. Having faith in God and an unfailing desire to help others, she always managed to elude her would-be captors. It is reported that at one time there was a $40,000 reward for her capture. Harriet became quite crafty at using disguises and by sending cryptic messages to signal her coming. Although she rescued most of her family, a most memorable occasion for her was when she liberated her aged parents.

During the Civil War, Harriet served the Union Army as scout, spy and nurse. In 1863, she led the Union Army on a raid which resulted in the freedom of over 750 slaves. After the war, she settled in Auburn, New York. She applied for a military pension but was forced to live in poverty for 30 years before it was granted. In 1897, Congress passed a private bill granting her $20 a month. She used the pension to establish the Harriet Tubman Home for Indigent Aged Negroes.

Harriet Ross Tubman lived to be 93. She was buried in Ohio with military honors in March, 1913. On June 12, 1914, in Auburn, New York, flags flew at half mast. Whites and Blacks gathered together by the thousands to pay tribute to the great contribution she made to her country and her people. In the words of Booker T. Washington, "She brought the two races together and made it possible for the White race to place a higher estimate on the Black race."

MADAME C. J. WALKER
1867-1919

Madame C. J. Walker (born Sarah Breed-love, on December 23, 1867) was America's first Black millionaire businesswoman. She achieved her success by discovering a new hair care process and marketing a line of toilet articles and cosmetics for Black women. She became the world's first Black woman of modern times to build a manufacturing business of great proportions.

Born to ex-slave parents in Delta, Louisiana, Sarah lost both parents, at age 6, and was reared by a married sister. She became Mrs. McWilliams at age 14, and bore a daughter, A'Lelia. By the time she reached 20, she was widowed.

In 1887, she moved to St. Louis, where she took in washing for 18 years to support herself, earning $1.50 a day. To educate herself, she attended night school. Sarah made a capital investment of one day's earning to start her experiments. Little did she know that this venture would make her the richest Black woman in the world.

With sore knuckles and a nearly broken back, she mixed one concoction after another in her washtub until she hit upon the right combination of oils. Her discovery resulted in a hairdressing formula which revolutionized the hair care industry and changed the looks of Black women. Although the oils conditioned and softened the hair, they did not remove the excessive curl of Blacks' hair. In 1905, she invented and patented a straightening comb which, when heated and used with her pomade, would transform stubborn, lusterless hair into shining smooth hair.

In 1906, she married Charles Joseph Walker, a newspaperman, and was known thereafter as Madame C. J. Walker. Initially, the "Walker Method" concept was ridiculed by Whites and Blacks alike, but she clung to her dream. The popularity of her products began to rise, and the "Walker Method" spread so rapidly that after one year, she was able to open an office and manufacturing headquarters in Denver. She traveled alone for two years, demonstrating her technique from door to door. So successful were her personal selling and mail order businesses that she soon opened a second office which was managed by her daughter in Philadelphia, in 1908. Later, both offices were consolidated in Indianapolis, Indiana where a plant was built which served as the center of the Walker empire.

By 1919, the Madame C. J. Walker Manufacturing Company stretched an entire city block and provided employment for over three thousand people. Walker's agents, whom Madame Walker called "hair, scalp and beauty culturists" became familiar figures throughout the United States and the Caribbean. Madame Walker, herself, made frequent instructional tours. She stressed "cleanliness and loveliness" as assets and as aids to self-respect and racial advance.

Her agents were required to sign contracts binding them to a hygienic regimen which eventually came to be incorporated into state cosmetology laws. She became one of the best-known Blacks in this Country and Europe. In the 1920s, the "Walker Method" coiffure of the celebrated Black dancer, Josephine Baker, fascinated the Parisians so much that a French company tried to produce a comparable product called "Baker-Fix."

A hard-driving saleswoman, Madame Walker was an exceedingly kind and generous benefactress of the Black community. She sponsored Black artists and writers and made sizable contributions to the needy, the NAACP, the YMCA, and homes for the aged. She awarded scholarships to young women at Tuskegee and Palmer Memorial Institutes, and supported the efforts of Mary McLeod Bethune and Ida B. Wells. She bequeathed $100,000 toward construction of an academy for girls in West Africa. She also provided in her will that two-thirds of the profits of her company would be allotted to charitable organizations.

Madame C. J. Walker died on May 25, 1919. At the time of her death, she had acquired a vast empire in excess of one million dollars. Among real estate holdings left to her daughter was a $250,000, 30-room mansion, Villa Lewaro, built in New York in 1917.

Maggie Lena Walker was the nation's first female bank president. She was organizer and founder of the St. Luke Bank and Trust company of Richmond, Virginia. Mrs. Walker came from an impoverished family, but her personal status and wealth grew tremendously over the years.

Maggie was born in 1867, one of two children, to William Mitchell and Elizabeth Draper, who had been slaves belonging to the well-known Van Lew family of Richmond. As a child, Maggie roamed through the gardens at the Van Lew mansion, which was a station on the Underground Railroad. Mistress Elizabeth Van Lew had been a notorious Union spy and harbored Union soldiers after they escaped from Confederate prisons in Richmond.

As a child, Maggie was a gifted student. She finished high school at the head of her class, at age 16, and began a teaching career. Shortly thereafter, she traded teaching for a position as executive secretary of the Independent Order of St. Luke Society. Within ten years, she was promoted to grand secretary-treasurer, a position she held for 35 years. Without any previous training, she achieved immediate success for the Order.

In the latter 1800s, insurance policies were unheard of for Blacks. The purpose of the Order of St. Luke was to assist sick and aged members, and provide funeral and burial services. Maggie maintained the membership records. Later, she conceived the notion of teaching members how to save and invest their money. From this idea grew her plan for founding St. Luke Penny Savings Bank, of which she became president.

When Maggie assumed the position of secretary-treasurer in 1899, the organization had about 3,400 members, but no reserve funds, no property, and an inadequate staff. By 1924, not only had she increased the membership to 100,000, but she had acquired a $100,000 office building, a cash reserve of about

$70,000 and a full-time working staff of 55, along with 145 field workers. Also, members could follow the course of her progress by reading the *St. Luke Herald* newspaper, another venture she launched. In September, 1890, Maggie married Armistead Walker, a well-to-do Black businessman. They had two sons. After the birth of their first son, Russell, Maggie put her care into the hands of household servants and devoted the majority of her time to the Order. She moved up in rank, establishing new services with each advancement. In 1895, she formed the Juvenile Branch of the Order and drafted governing laws. Her second son, Melvin, was born in 1897.

In 1903, Walker instigated the important move of changing the name of the St. Luke Penny Savings Bank to the St. Luke Bank and Trust Company. Later, it became the Consolidated Bank and Trust Company, with Walker as chairman of the board. Maggie Walker made giant strides in her lifetime, a solid citizen respected by Whites and Blacks alike. She organized and stood at the helm of many civic organizations; the St. Luke Educational Fund to help Black boys and girls get an education, organizer and president of the Council of Colored Women. She was a trustee of the National Training School in Washington, D.C., a national director of the NAACP, board member of the National Urban League, and an appointee of various governors of Virginia.

Maggie Walker was also the prime mover in the establishment of a home for delinquent Black girls in Richmond. She organized 1,400 women into a council which paid the first $5,000 to purchase land for the institution. She was prominent in all community enterprises and was the recipient of several honorary degrees.

Blacks paid her a great honor in 1934, when national Black organizations declared the month of October "Maggie L. Walker Month." One thousand statuettes of her were placed in Black homes, schools, and businesses across the country. She died later that same year.

She became a pioneer in literary history, a poetess of the American Revolution, and the first Black female poetess in the United States. She was Phillis Wheatley.

On an ordinary day in 1761, a ship docked in the Boston harbor bearing a most precious cargo. Somewhere buried in its hull was a little slave girl of unknown origin. Some say she was from Ethiopia; others say, Senegal, West Africa. Judging from the loss of her first teeth, she could have been between the ages of 6 and 8. She was of no known parentage, since slave captors did not record vital statistics—yet she was to leave her mark upon the chronicles of time.

Phillis Wheatley stood on the auction block, thin and frail, terrified, not understanding the noisy crowd of buyers surrounding her. Her small hand clutched at the dirty, scanty piece of cloth half hiding her nakedness, when suddenly a strange but gentle hand led her to a carriage, wherein she was greeted by a warm, smiling face. She had been purchased by John Wheatley, a wealthy merchant tailor, for his wife Susannah. Mrs. Wheatley had been so touched by the pathetic appearance and modest look of this little Black girl that she could not fight the swell of compassion in her heart.

Once at the Wheatley home, Phillis was treated as a daughter and assigned chores relative to the status of a lady. Mrs. Wheatley referred to her as "my Phillis." Phillis was taught to read and write by the Wheatleys' son and daughter. In a short time, they learned that Phillis possessed an unusual precocity. Within sixteen months of her arrival, she had attained the English Language to such a degree as to read any, the most difficult parts of the sacred writings. She learned geography and history and became quite proficient in Latin. She was a privileged person. At age 14, she began writing poetry. It was not long before knowledge of this gifted slave girl attracted the attention of the most distinguished Bostonians.

In 1770, Phillis wrote her first published poem—"On the Death of the Rev. Mr. George Whitefield," a eulogy, which came to the attention of the Countess of Huntington in England. Three years later, when Phillis was sent to England for reasons of health, the Countess introduced her to the Lord Mayor and other members of nobility. Phillis so impressed the noble crowd of England that before she left, the Countess had arranged to have a volume of her poems published.

In 1773, the first book of poems by an American Black woman came off the press. It consisted of *Poems on Various Subjects, Religious* and *Moral*. To prove Phillis' authorship, a foreword attesting to Phillis' talent was signed by eighteen prominent Massachusetts men, including the wealthy merchant John Hancock and the governor of the colony. Just before Phillis was to be presented at Court, she received word that her mistress was deathly ill. She hurried home after one month of historic success.

Good fortune soon gave way to misfortune. Her mistress died in 1774, and her master died in 1778. Phillis became a free person, in the sense that she was not owned, but she became an instant slave of hard times, sadness, and a life of poverty. The Revolutionary War changed her life as well as others. One month after the death of John Wheatley, she married a pseudo-gentleman by the name of John Peters. Peters was not a good provider, and Phillis was forced to work as a servant. She bore two children, who died almost immediately after birth.

Phillis' health failed, and soon death came for her and her third child. She and the child died within hours of each other on December 5, 1784. Just before she died, she wrote a long poem entitled *Liberty and Peace*.

TEST YOURSELF

Now that you have familiarized yourself with our historic Black women in this first series of Empak's Black History Month promotion, this section, in three parts: MATCH, TRUE/FALSE, MULTIPLE CHOICE/FILL-IN, is designed to help you remember some key points about each notable Black woman. (Answers on page 32)

MATCH

I. *Match the column on the right with the column on the left by placing the appropriate alphabetical letter next to the person's name it represents.*

1. Elizabeth Taylor-Greenfield_____
2. Frances Ellen Harper_____
3. Mary Ann Shadd Cary_____
4. Harriet Ross Tubman_____
5. Mary Church Terrell_____
6. Mary E. Bowser_____
7. Ellen Craft_____
8. Florence B. Price_____

A) Moses of her people
B) Master of Disguise
C) Champion of women's rights
D) Union Spy
E) Black Swan
F) Composer
G) Bronze Muse
H) Swedish Nightingale
I) The Rebel

TRUE/FALSE

II. *The True and False statements below are taken from the biographical information given on each historic Black woman.*

1. Ida B. Wells wrote a statistical account on lynchings in the United States called "A Red Record." _____
2. Phillis Wheatley was the first Black American woman to write a novel._____
3. Mary Eliza Mahoney was the first Black graduate nurse in the United States._____
4. Nina Mae McKinney was the first recognized Black actress in the "silver screen."_____
5. Bessie Coleman attended one of the best aviation schools in the United States._____
6. Frances Ellen Harper is the first published Black woman poet._____
7. Madame C.J. Walker is noted as the first female bank president._____
8. Mary McLeod Bethune is the first Black woman to establish a four-year college. _____

MULTIPLE CHOICE/FILL-IN

III. *Complete the statements below by drawing a line under the correct name, or by filling-in the correct answer which you have read in the biographical sketches.*

1. (Crystal Fauset, Ella Phillips Stewart, Mary Ann Cary) was the first Black female elected to the Pennsylvania State Legislature.
2. _____ is noted as a financial genius and the "mother of the civil rights struggle in California."
3. The statement, "I, too can make a stone man," was made by the first noted Black woman sculptress (Mary E. Bowser, Mary E. Lewis, Mary E. Mahoney).
4. One of these pioneers in medicine was the first Black woman dentist in the United States (Ida Gray, Ella Phillips Stewart, Susan McKinney Steward).
5. _____, an advocate of abolition and equality for the "lesser sex," wore a banner across her chest proclaiming freedom for all inhabitants.
6. The oldest living Black woman pharmacist in the U.S. is _____.
7. The noted educator who founded the National Trade and Professional School for Women and Girls was (Mary Church Terrell, Mary McLeod Bethune, Nannie Helen Burroughs.)
8. _____ was the first Black newspaper woman on the North American continent. She was also the second Black woman lawyer in the U.S.

CROSSWORD PUZZLE

ACROSS

3. Courageous journalist
5. "I never lost a passenger..."
6. *Provincial Freeman* newspaper
10. Wanamaker Music Contest winner
11. Private-duty
12. Founded a Florida college
15. Love goddess
18. House of two-thirds vote
21. Over-the-counter remedies
22. Literary history pioneer

DOWN

1. Advocate of "three B's"
2. Infiltrated Confederate White House
3. As easy as pulling teeth
4. Master William Johnson
7. Eagle-winged
8. An astonishing range of notes
9. "Ain't I a woman?"
10. John Brown's alleged backer
13. *Iola Leroy or Shadows Uplifted*
14. Cosmetic inventor and manufacturer
16. Marble mastery
17. $$$$ Overseer
19. Honor grad from N.Y. medical college
20. Classical language exper

WORDSEARCH

1. Mary McLeod Bethune
2. Mary Bowser
3. Nannie H. Burroughs
4. Mary Ann Cary
5. Bessie Coleman
6. Ellen Craft
7. Crystal B. Fauset
8. Ida Gray
9. Elizabeth Greenfield
10. Frances Harper
11. Mary Edmonia Lewis
12. Mary Eliza Mahoney
13. Nina Mae McKinney
14. Mary Ellen Pleasant
15. Florence Price
16. Susan McKinney Steward
17. Ella Phillips Stewart
18. Mazy Church Terrell
19. Sojourner Truth
20. Harriet Tubman
21. Madame Walker
22. Maggie Walker
23. Ida B. Wells
24. Phillis Wheatley

The names of our twenty-four HISTORIC BLACK WOMEN are contained in the diagram below. Look in the diagram of letters for the names given in the list. Find the names by reading FORWARD, BACKWARDS, UP, DOWN, and DIAGONALLY in a straight line of letters. Each time you find a name in the diagram, circle it in the diagram and cross it off on the list of names. Words often overlap, and letters may be used more than once.

```
P H I L L I S W H E A T L E Y D I A O S H G Q I L A E E
O W D F O L A C N O M A R Y E D M O N I A L E W I S L L
E B A S R V T F E A R V S P K D D E M D S G A I M L I I
T E G V T N A S A E L P N E L L E Y R A M X D N A O R Z
E A R A A A T A O D O C T O R J T M Z B R E S P R T E A
S V A B B U M A R Y B O W S E R A L N W I G H I Y G D B
S B Y O E S I E C O L E M R N E Q Y D E E I H B M A R E
G S K T S T M W A Z R L K G Q A R S A L L H Y N C O A T
R U A B S W K T E C I R P E C N E R O L F Q E Z L Y W H
D A V A I H R G I Q V B K A G N Q I I S T S N P E C E G
E R T Y E W E O R M L S W O C S V P F O R T N V O Z T R
T F A R C N E L L E G E L T I S S N K I L R I F D A S E
M T O E O C Q H L T U V O N Y S E S T X E R K B B Z Y E
B E T H L S M L E K J I A H T D C A B K P O C N E R E N
S S C V E R E S R W C M F E M R X P L E F C M I T J N F
O K R O M R D U R A B G W D U Y L A O S T Z E D H B N I
J U Y R A L A G E U Q A F G K S W R N V Y X A G U C I E
O K S G N X D B T H R A I B L E N E E I U M M S N O K L
U I T J K S S T H T J C O E I M U W I P S N A I E L C D
R Z A Y X W E V C C H U G G G S U R V A E C N R S T M B
N H L I N I E A R D K P G W Y E C M O P O G I F K L N T
E I B C R P E J U L U A C O A T G R M A H B N A N A A O
R K F R Y E N O H A M A Z I L E Y R A M B E S S I X S W
T A A B D F C G C E H I J L O B A C M N P X W S J Z U N
R H U L A T I T Y S O N A N N I E H B U R R O U G H S L
U H S K E E T F R A N C E S H A R P E R H E R O N O E G
T A E R M A R Y A N N C A R Y H C A R A X W Q D N E B Y
H S T O S E A R M A D A M E W A L K E R H A G K S R N O
```

59

CROSSWORD PUZZLE

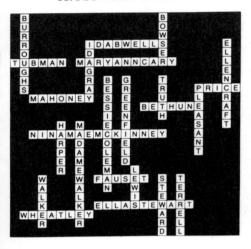

WORD SEARCH

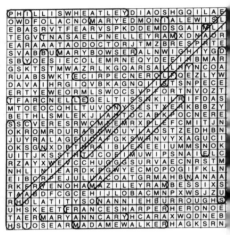

MATCH

1.–E	5.–C
2.–G	6.–D
3.–I	7.–B
4.–A	8.–F

TRUE/FALSE

1.–TRUE	5.–FALSE
2.–FALSE	6.–FALSE
3.–TRUE	7.–FALSE
4.–TRUE	8.–TRUE

MULTIPLE CHOICE/FILL IN

1. CRYSTAL FAUSET
2. MARY ELLEN PLEASANT
3. MARY E. LEWIS
4. IDA GRAY
5. SOJOURNER TRUTH
6. ELLA PHILLIPS STEWART
7. NANNIE HELEN BURROUGHS
8. MARY ANN CARY

Send to: Empak Publishing Company, 212 E. Ohio St., Suite 300, Chicago, IL 60611—Phone: (312) 642-8364

Name _____

Affiliation _____

Address _____
P. O. Box numbers not accepted, street address must appear.

City _____ State _____ Zip _____

Phone# (_____)_____ Date _____

Method Of Payment Enclosed:　　( ) Check　　　　( ) Money Order　　　　( ) Purchase Order

Prices effective 11/1/96 thru 10/31/97

ADVANCED LEVEL

Quantity	ISBN #	Title Description	Unit Price	Total Price
	0-922162-1-8	"A Salute to Historic Black Women"		
	0-922162-2-6	"A Salute to Black Scientists & Inventors"		
	0-922162-3-4	"A Salute to Black Pioneers"		
	0-922162-4-2	"A Salute to Black Civil Rights Leaders"		
	0-922162-5-0	"A Salute to Historic Black Abolitionists"		
	0-922162-6-9	"A Salute to Historic African Kings & Queens"		
	0-922162-7-7	"A Salute to Historic Black Firsts"		
	0-922162-8-5	"A Salute to Historic Blacks in the Arts"		
	0-922162-9-3	"A Salute to Blacks in the Federal Government"		
	0-922162-14-X	"A Salute to Historic Black Educators"		

INTERMEDIATE LEVEL

	0-922162-75-1	"Historic Black Women"		
	0-922162-76-X	"Black Scientists & Inventors"		
	0-922162-77-8	"Historic Black Pioneers"		
	0-922162-78-6	"Black Civil Rights Leaders"		
	0-922162-80-8	"Historic Black Abolitionists"		
	0-922162-81-6	"Historic African Kings & Queens"		
	0-922162-82-4	"Historic Black Firsts"		
	0-922162-83-2	"Historic Blacks in the Arts"		
	0-922162-84-0	"Blacks in the Federal Government"		
	0-922162-85-9	"Historic Black Educators"		

Total Books			❸ Subtotal	
			❹ IL Residents add 8.75% Sales Tax	
	SEE ABOVE CHART ▷		❺ Shipping & Handling	
GRADE LEVEL: 4th, 5th, 6th			❻ Total	

BOOK PRICING ● QUANTITY DISCOUNTS

Advanced Level	Intermediate Level
Reg. $3.49	Reg. $2.29
Order 50 or More	Order 50 or More
Save 40¢ EACH	Save 20¢ EACH
@ $3.09	@ $2.09

❺ SHIPPING AND HANDLING

Order Total	Add
Under $5.00	$1.50
$5.01-$15.00	$3.00
$15.01-$35.00	$4.50
$35.01-$75.00	$7.00
$75.01-$200.00	10%
Over $201.00	6%

In addition to the above charges, U.S. territories, HI & AK, add $2.00. Canada & Mexico, add $5.00. Other outside U.S., add $20.00.

EPC

Name _____

Affiliation _____

Street _____
P. O. Box numbers not accepted, street address must appear.

City _____ State _____ Zip _____

Phone (_____)_____ Date _____

Method Of Payment Enclosed: ( ) Check   ( ) Money Order   ( ) Purchase Order

Prices effective 11/1/96 thru 10/31/97

PRIMARY LEVEL... KINDERGARTEN, FIRST, SECOND & THIRD GRADE

Quantity	ISBN #	Title Description	Unit Price	Total Price
	0-922162-90-5	"Kumi and Chanti"		
	0-922162-91-3	"George Washington Carver"		
	0-922162-92-1	"Harriet Tubman"		
	0-922162-93-X	"Jean Baptist DuSable"		
	0-922162-94-8	"Matthew Henson"		
	0-922162-95-6	"Bessie Coleman"		
Total Books			❸ Subtotal	
			❹ IL Residents add 8.75% Sales Tax	
		SEE CHART BELOW ▷	❺ Shipping & Handling	
			❻ Total	

KEY STEPS IN ORDERING

❶ Establish quantity needs.   ❹ Add tax, if applicable.
❷ Determine book unit price.   ❺ Add shipping &handling.
❸ Determine total cost.   ❻ Total amount.

BOOK PRICING ● QUANTITY DISCOUNTS

❶ Quantity Ordered	❷ Unit Price
1-49	$3.49
50 +	$3.09

❺ SHIPPING AND HANDLING

Order Total	Add
Under $5	$1.50
$5.01-$15.00	$3.00
$15.01- $35.00	$4.50
$35.01-$75.00	$7.00
$75.01-$200.00	10%
Over $201.00	6%

In addition to the above charges, U.S. territories, HI & AK, add $2.00. Canada and Mexico, add $5.00. Other outside U.S., add $20.00.

Empak Publishing provides attractive counter and floor displays for retailers and organizations interested in the Heritage book series for resale. Please check here ☐ and include this form with your letterhead and we will send you specific information and our special volume discounts.

- The Empak "Heritage Kids" series provides a basic understanding and appreciation of Black history which translates to cultural awareness, self-esteem, and ethnic pride within young African-American children.

- Assisted by dynamic and impressive 4-color illustrations, readers will be able to relate to the two adorable African kids-- Kumi & Chanti, as they are introduced to the inspirational lives and deeds of significant, historic African-Americans.

Helps for Translators Series

Technical Helps:

Old Testament Quotations in the New Testament
Section Headings for the New Testament
Short Bible Reference System
New Testament Index
Orthography Studies
Bible Translations for Popular Use
The Theory and Practice of Translation
Bible Index
Fauna and Flora of the Bible
Manuscript Preparation
Marginal Notes for the Old Testament
Marginal Notes for the New Testament
The Practice of Translating

Handbooks:

A Translator's Handbook on the Book of Joshua
A Translator's Handbook of the Book of Ruth
A Translator's Handbook on the Book of Amos
A Translator's Handbook on the Books of Obadiah and Micah
A Translator's Handbook on the Book of Jonah
A Translator's Handbook on the Gospel of Mark
A Translator's Handbook on the Gospel of Luke
A Translator's Handbook on the Gospel of John
A Translator's Handbook on the Acts of the Apostles
A Translator's Handbook on Paul's First Letter to the Corinthians
A Translator's Handbook on Paul's Letter to the Romans
A Translator's Handbook on Paul's Letter to the Galatians
A Translator's Handbook on Paul's Letter to the Ephesians
A Translator's Handbook on Paul's Letter to the Philippians
A Translator's Handbook on Paul's Letters to the Colossians and to Philemon
A Translator's Handbook on Paul's Letters to the Thessalonians
A Translator's Handbook on the Letter to the Hebrews
A Translator's Handbook on the First Letter from Peter
A Translator's Handbook on the Letters of John

Guides:

A Translator's Guide to Selections from the First Five Books of the Old Testament
A Translator's Guide to Selected Psalms
A Translator's Guide to the Gospel of Matthew
A Translator's Guide to the Gospel of Mark
A Translator's Guide to the Gospel of Luke
A Translator's Guide to Paul's First Letter to the Corinthians
A Translator's Guide to Paul's Letters to Timothy and to Titus
A Translator's Guide to the Letters to James, Peter, and Jude
A Translator's Guide to the Revelation to John

A TRANSLATORS HANDBOOK
ON PAUL'S LETTER TO
THE PHILIPPIANS